# GIFTS

## ROBERT D. GRAPPEL

Copyright 2023 by Robert Grappel

ISBN:   979-8-9891452-8-7 (Paperback)
        979-8-9896648-6-3 (Hardback)
        979-8-9891452-9-4 (Ebook)

All rights reserved. No part of this publication may be reproduced, distributed, or transmitted in any form or by any means, including photocopying, recording, or other electronic or mechanical methods, without the prior written permission of the publisher, except in the case brief quotations embodied in critical reviews and other noncommercial uses permitted by copyright law.

The views expressed in this book are solely those of the author and do not necessarily reflect the views of the publisher, and the publisher hereby disclaims any responsibility for them.

Olympus Story House

# List of Poems

Zichronot – Remembrances . . . . . . . . . . . . . . . . . . . . . . . . . 3
The Binding. . . . . . . . . . . . . . . . . . . . . . . . . . . . . . . . . . . . . . 5
The Painted Potsherd. . . . . . . . . . . . . . . . . . . . . . . . . . . . . . 8
Hinter Aedige (Behind the Cathedral) . . . . . . . . . . . . . . . 10
Detroit Metro Fantasy . . . . . . . . . . . . . . . . . . . . . . . . . . . . 12
Total Eclipse . . . . . . . . . . . . . . . . . . . . . . . . . . . . . . . . . . . . 14
Images of Portugal . . . . . . . . . . . . . . . . . . . . . . . . . . . . . . . 17
For Lynda. . . . . . . . . . . . . . . . . . . . . . . . . . . . . . . . . . . . . . . 19
Dedication. . . . . . . . . . . . . . . . . . . . . . . . . . . . . . . . . . . . . . 20
The Pantheon . . . . . . . . . . . . . . . . . . . . . . . . . . . . . . . . . . . 21
Murano Glass . . . . . . . . . . . . . . . . . . . . . . . . . . . . . . . . . . . 22
Bonita Flakes. . . . . . . . . . . . . . . . . . . . . . . . . . . . . . . . . . . . 23
The Day I Became 23 . . . . . . . . . . . . . . . . . . . . . . . . . . . . 24
Kol Nidrei . . . . . . . . . . . . . . . . . . . . . . . . . . . . . . . . . . . . . . 26
A Stone in the Stream . . . . . . . . . . . . . . . . . . . . . . . . . . . . 28
The Layer-Cake Country. . . . . . . . . . . . . . . . . . . . . . . . . . 29
Old Blue Jeans. . . . . . . . . . . . . . . . . . . . . . . . . . . . . . . . . . . 31
The Trouble with Corners . . . . . . . . . . . . . . . . . . . . . . . . 33
A Modern "U'va Shofar Godol" . . . . . . . . . . . . . . . . . . . . 35
Bible Study. . . . . . . . . . . . . . . . . . . . . . . . . . . . . . . . . . . . . . 37
Conception . . . . . . . . . . . . . . . . . . . . . . . . . . . . . . . . . . . . . 39
California Sunrise. . . . . . . . . . . . . . . . . . . . . . . . . . . . . . . . 40
Sunrise Colors. . . . . . . . . . . . . . . . . . . . . . . . . . . . . . . . . . . 41
Why I Don't "Get" Jackson Pollock . . . . . . . . . . . . . . . . . 42

The Evolution of Fear.............................. 44
Is The Jar Full Yet? ................................ 46
A Stain on Stained Glass .......................... 47
Certainty ........................................ 48

# GIFTS

Robert D. Grappel

The poems in this book came to me as gifts. They appeared almost fully formed in my consciousness – I had only to write them down before they could vanish back into the void where beauty is born. I have done some editing and smoothing of the rough edges – wrapping these gifts in shiny paper and tying them with a silken bow. I hope you enjoy them.

I'd like to thank my wife, Lynda, for her steadfast love, continuing support, and for sharing many of the experiences that inspired these poems. Thanks to Teal Sallen of *Blue Waterfall Productions*, who shared her artistic gifts and talent to create the cover art and internal illustrations for this book. Thanks to Julia O'Doherty Walker of *By Design Photography* who made me look distinguished. I must acknowledge my parents who first read poems to me and then endured listening to my initial efforts. To a long series of English teachers – I hope you were not too discouraged with your student.

© 2007, Robert D. Grappel

# Zichronot – Remembrances

*This poem was written during a trip to Israel in 2000. I was walking on the shore in the resort city of Eilat on Israel's "independence day". Precisely at noon, the sirens signal a minute of remembrance – an extremely moving experience. Fortunately, I had enough room on the margins of my city map to write this down.*

An air-raid siren screams,
The twenty-first century Shofar
And all Israel stops – holds its breath – and remembers…
The sleeping death in its bunkers under Dimona…
The soldiers in their tanks along the Negev…
The tourists on the ocean walk of Eilat.

For a moment we all stand like statues.
Only the sea and air continue to move,
For they have no need to remember
In this land more ancient than histories
Yet younger than many of her people.

We remember – each in our own way
Those who died in terror and ugliness far away
Dreaming of a golden land they would never see.
Some who gave their young lives in this new country
Dreaming of families and children scant minutes away.

The Israeli soldier puts down his rifle above the western wall,
Picks up his cellular phone, and smiles.
The Egyptian border guard leaves his sentry tower above the Sinai
To pose by a tour bus and the razor wire.
The worker piling soda cans, the shop keepers…
They each keep a memory.
And those memories live on in this land
As surely as the people who share her bounty.

The siren's wail drops to a hush – a moment more of silence
The world begins to turn again – a new day
The memories renewed.
May this be our prayer in all the world…
Next year – when the sirens wail,
When the land of Israel stops,
Holds its breath again…
May we have no one else to remember.

# The Binding

*This poem is based on the Biblical story of Abraham being asked to sacrifice his only son, Isaac, to God. Traditionally read as part of the celebration of the Jewish New Year, the narrative contrasts a father's love with the stories of modern "sacrifices" about which we read all too often in the daily newspaper.*

*Abraham wrapped his robe about him,*
*Laced his sandals upon his feet,*
*Took his staff in his hand,*
*And started off down the path*
*To the place of which God had told him.*

> A young man rises early one cool morning
> Washes himself and says the prayers,
> Stuffs bricks of explosives inside his down vest,
> Takes the detonator in his hand,
> And walks off toward the border checkpoint.

*Isaac said to his father Abraham,*
*"I see the wood and the fire,*
*But where is the lamb for our sacrifice?"*

> A pretty young girl with a smiling face
> Her spirit fierce as the desert sun
> Puts on a girdle of dynamite sticks
> Wraps colored wires about her

Like an embroidered shawl
And stands waiting for a crowded bus.

*And Abraham stretched forth his hand*
*And took the knife to slay his son*

> An aged man goes every day to the local mosque
> To teach the children how bombs are made.
> How a timer is set, how a charge is wired.
> How a grenade is launched, how a machine gun fired.
> Who to hate and who to kill,
> And why "the cause" is worth the dying.

*But the angel of God called out to Abraham,*
*And Abraham responded, "Here am I".*
*"Do not lay your hand on Isaac, your son,*
*For I can see that your faith is strong.*
*I will make of you a great nation.*
*Through you all the world shall be blessed."*

> God calls us too, from beyond the centuries.
> Do not kill your children to prove your faith in Me.
> Do not take away the lives I have given you.
> Use your time on Earth for nurturing,
> Creating, and growing.
> Hearken to My voice!

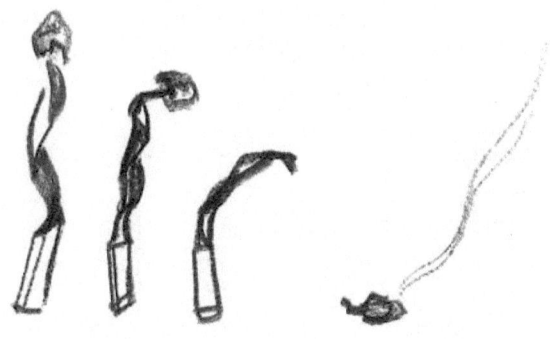

# The Painted Potsherd

*This poem was originally written for a college English class. The inspiration was a display of ancient Greek and Egyptian pottery in the university museum. Another inspiration was a medieval poem picturing God as a potter, forming people from dust and clay. A later revision of this poem was helped along by a poetry workshop.*


The water jar shatters
Simon the Meek
Rushing out from the encircling fold
Takes arms against silent foes
Ready in murmuring grass blades
In the shimmering heat – sky dripping tears as a salty dew
Upon gleaming sand like stars in a mirror…
Thoughts
The plants sway like mourners – the wind rushing on
Sees the painted figures,
Two dimensions of clay and paint
All dust.

Sheep eat grass
And clay moldering in wet, sticky sand
Yields itself to brooding time
With many cracking groans of protest…
Paint flakes cry softly,
And the earthworm carves his home in rich soil
Heavy with men's work.

Mature hands once formed the spinning mass – once painted it
Tilled this soil,
Now sow destruction and harvest crops of blood.
Claret pigment mixes with the media
Still dust.

The breakers roar their challenges in diamonds
Shining green upon a rock…
The answer to the sea
Clashes like many sword blades in battle.
The sun dries tears of mourning
Clear crystals of love remain
And peaceful sheep may trod the ancient battlefields
Buried as corpses without a coffin.
Simon returns to his flock older and wiser.
He throws down his shield
Upon the ground
Deep in dust.

Simon the Meek holds dust.
The Heavens pour the water,
And by the rushing stream he begins again
To fashion the vessel – bronze girt and large enough
To hold the sorrows of nations
Making the dust cry out when Simon struck them
And spilled water on their unmarked graves.
Simon the Meek…
A rare man in his day.
He peered through the windows of truth.
He knocked on the great, white gate.
He asked his questions
Of the dust.

# Hinter Aedige
# (Behind the Cathedral)

*In the town of Braunschweig, in northeastern Germany, there is a Jewish Museum. It contains the interior of a 19th century German synagogue that survived the devastation of World War II by being sealed over with a layer of concrete. The museum is now housed in the basement of an unused monastery building attached to one of Braunschweig's imposing stone churches, some of which date back to the 1100's.*

A 12th century church in Braunschweig, Germany...
Moss and ivy cover the piled stony walls
Whose lead-rimmed windows watched Crusaders pass.
My fathers wrenched these rocks from southern mountains
And watched the armored figures glinting in reflected sunlight.
Bright banners hanging from the northern spires
Heard the cheering crowds bid their heroes "Godspeed"
As the people walked back to tend their fields.

In a basement room behind the vaulted sanctuary
Through carved oak doors, down timeworn stairs
Generations of monks toiled silently through the centuries.
Maintaining the memories of my fathers resting
Asleep beneath their plowed-earth fields.

This room once filled with prayer and song,
Flickering candles and shuffling feet.
My fathers read out the law from parchment scrolls
Draped with velvet mantles and silver crowned.
Now silent, my footsteps lonely echo
Amid the photographs and embroidery.

This fragment of history freed from its concrete tomb
Like people's minds now open to long hidden thoughts.
They hewed these beams and quarried these stones
And now remember the world that died here.

# Detroit Metro Fantasy

*This poem was written while flying back to the University of Michigan for the winter semester. Most of the images were seen from my window during the landing approach.*

Cities lie below in the hazy night.
Shining crystals of soft snow falling
Across the gently-lit path
Glowing instruments
As the landing gear drops into place.
Airports loom suddenly in the blackness.
Dream fingers reach up
And I glide in easy.

The glowing golden mists surround me.
My fuzzy, silver-feathered wings rustle low.
My hands sweat on the controls ...
Sky, landing lights, and all swirl in reverie.
I long to forget everything.
The Christmas lights mark my wingtips -- cannot bind me.
I feel the wings within!

Scrunch!
The runway groans with the landing shock.
Shattered dreams, awakening slumber.
"You are not a bird!
The earth claims its own!"

I know...
Windshield glass forms prison bars
Across the ever-grays of stars.

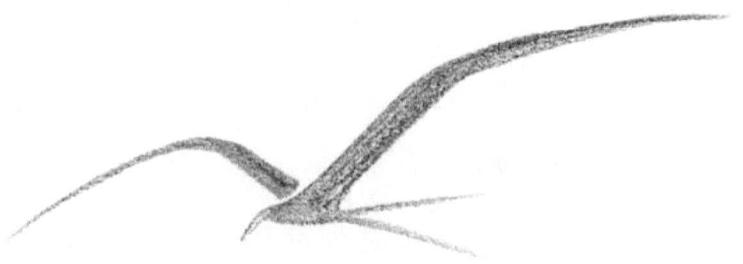

# Total Eclipse

*In Exodus Chapter 33, Moses asks to see God face-to-face in order to solidify his faith. This from a man who, the Bible tells us, converses directly with God repeatedly! Who saw the plagues of Egypt first-hand! Who watched the sea part under his outstretched staff! God tells Moses that no human can look directly at the face of God and survive, but God will place Moses in a sheltered place behind a rock and cover him with His hand so that Moses will only see His back. I wonder what it would take to secure my faith...*

It was a brilliant summer's morning
The sunshine dazzling in a cloudless sky.
Green leaves rustled in a cooling breeze
While birds sang hymns to a bright blue day.

The moon meanwhile swung in orbit about the Earth,
A tiny rock adrift in the blazing solar glare.
For a moment its shadow raced across the land.
The eclipse had begun.

    Moses said, "God, I need more help to believe."
    And God replied, "I have shown you signs and wonders,
    Brought your people through the sea to safety,
    Yet still your faith in Me wavers."

At first it is only a feeling -- a sensation that is somehow different.
The colors changing hue -- the sky darkens and the stars appear.
The birds fall silent and Nature holds its breath
This is no normal sunset.

> And God said, "I will shelter you behind a rock
> So that My Glory will not destroy you.
> I will place My hand before your eyes
> So that My shadow will not burn you."

A purple shadow covers the sun.
While people stand by watching – amazed.
Bright beads of pearly light rim the moon.
Then suddenly wink out -- the eclipse is total.

Solar corona flames appear in their celestial glory.
Streamers reaching out for thousands of miles
More vast than all the space we can inhabit,
As we dare to look upon it.

An eclipse lasts just a few minutes
Only a breath in the passage of eternal time.
The sky brightens and Nature resumes its way.
Another miracle that God has shown us.

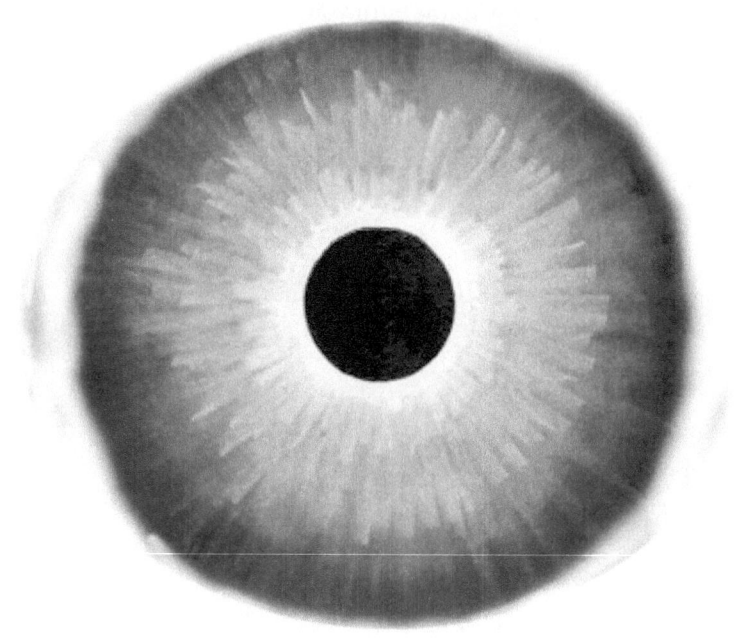

# Images of Portugal

*This poem resulted from a bus tour of Portugal. My wife and I spent a week in this most-amazing and picturesque country.*

The ancient country sits hunched on the mountains
Like a crouching beast,
With granite spine and marble ribs
Growing warm in the morning sun.

Stairways for giants rise along the hillsides of the Douro
Where Roman sentries once kept watch from fortress walls
And Visigoths threw down these stones
To lie unnoticed beside the river.
Covered by the growth of generations.
Vineyard, cork tree, man...
All living side-by-side here
Mindless of the centuries passing.

The sea crashes upon the sand below the cliffs at Nazarre'.
The echoes of Phoenician seamen's cries
Mixed with the mew of gulls and diesel rumbling.
Bright-colored boats with upswept prows and painted eyes
See these same proud, wave-tossed waters
Which fed their great-grandfathers.
While new generations of sardine and cod
Await the sons of these fishermen.

A vineyard climbs high to reach the noonday sun
Above a tiny terraced garden in the Minho.
No spot of earth too small here
To support a bunch of grapes -- a family
Which has seen Moors and Spaniards come and go
In the unending succession of plant and harvest.

The green wine, *Vinho Verde*, goes by ox-cart to a table at Lamego
Past hillsides of eucalyptus trees
Silver shimmer interwoven with orange, olive, and oak
Like filigree made by the craftsmen
Who carry their goods to the sea at Oporto.
Newcomers, centuries old, share their fields
With kale and fava beans.

Women in the market wear seven petticoats
In colors of the rainbow arc over sun-splashed cliffs
Mirrored in the scales of a thousand fishes
Drying in the shore-side marketplace
While flowers in profusion scale the ramparts
Vanquishing the ancient walls of Obidos.

Oak trees form the ribs for fishing trawlers
Pine planked with craftsmanship older than the trees.
Stouthearted ships, like the men who build and man them.
This country has a deep keel -- buried deep in her mountains.
She feels the warm sun and the salt spray...
The sweat of farmers working the land their grandfathers knew...
and the souls of many peoples who came to love her...

# For Lynda

*I wrote this poem as a gift for my wife in 1992.*

I'm thinking of you
As I often do
When work is done.

How you bring light
And widening sight
To our joys just begun.

Our lives have a meaning
Beyond frantic scheming
In the harsh daytime sun.

So shall we give,
Each to the other
Love, beyond sister or brother,
In all days to come.

# Dedication

*This poem was written for the dedication service of our congregation's new Temple building in 2002. Many of the images came from my "unique" perspective as a long-time choir member looking out and up.*

Children's laughter in a framework of steel
Where plaster and wood hold jubilant songs
Sweet music of choirs -- a bride's blushing "I do"
A Bar Mitzvah davening -- Ne'ilah's final "Amen"
Murmur of mourner's Kaddish -- a silent Amidah
Tinkling Torah crowns -- echoes of Shofar sounds
Room for growing families in glass and bronze
Foundation forged from many hearts.

Velvet and glass see our tears and joys
Chatter of friends greeting from the tiles and doors
Prayers of the faithful upon concrete and stone
While Shabbat candles flicker in the gathering night
Soft flower fragrance in white silk arrayed
Sweet tastes of Kiddush -- in community shared -- "L'Chayim!"
The old and the new now joined in harmonious whole
Generations look down lovingly from the skylights -- smiling.

# The Pantheon

*This poem came to me during a trip to Italy in 2004. Lynda and I were touring the Pantheon in Rome – an amazing structure, both massive and airy at the same time. Among the tourists in our group was a traveling German choir who decided to do an impromptu concert in the marvelous acoustics of the great hall.*

"Pan Theus" – a temple for all the gods
The home of peoples from all the Earth
All the tourists – all the ages
Sky – a perfect sphere,
Above an imperfect world.

Built to crown an emperor's glory
A monument throughout the centuries
Amidst the teeming traffic's hum
A choir's "amen" echoes.

# Murano Glass

*The city of Venice, Italy, has been the center of the glassmaker's art for nearly a millennium. The secrets of forming and coloring glass were closely held by Venetian crafts guilds. In the early 1500's, Jewish refugees from the Inquisition in Spain and Portugal (called "Marano's") came to Venice and some became glassmakers on the island called "Murano". This tradition continues to the present day.*

Sand…
Mixed with Adriatic salt
Watered with the craftsman's tears
Fired in the furnace heat
Of a Venetian summer
On Murano – island of his exile.

Cobalt blue reminders of Spanish seas
Mixed with the Doge's gold
Copper green like a Portuguese hillside
In earlier days.

A puff of breath…
A fragile bubble forms
Clearest crystal in his mind and hands
A pull, a tug, a twist, a swing of the pipe
A horse emerges from the glass
As though already there.

# Bonita Flakes

*I wrote this poem during a trip to Kobe, Japan. Bonita Flakes are a popular Japanese condiment. The Japanese like to shake them onto hot noodles and other dishes. Shaved from dried fish, they tend to wiggle and writhe in the steam rising from your meal.*

No, they're not
Some Japanese breakfast cereal...
Looking like fresh wood shavings
Curled from a carpenter's plane.

Rather -- bits of dried fish, long from the sea,
Beat their tiny fly wings, fan the air,
Wriggle on my plate of steamed soba
Noodles in a seaweed broth...
Remembering the rolling waves
That washed once on the Kobe shore.
An acquired taste...
The Japanese love.
I think not!

# The Day I Became 23

*I had no recollection of writing this poem until I found it in my old files. I was in my first year of graduate school, and my father was about to retire after recovering from his second heart attack. The poem reads like self-psychiatric therapy to me now. Little did I realize that within 6 months of writing this I'd be engaged.*

Mommy won't let me go outside
After the darkness comes.
She says I'll get hurt on the swings
And she can't come out and see
If I'm hurt
Bleeding through the skin.

Maybe I might cross the streets
Of our block
And lose myself in the wide worlds
Which are lost to her.

The stars could fall on me.
I'd pick them up off the dirty sidewalk
Like the Halloween candy
When my bag broke
With the razor blades it tried to hide
Scattered helter-skelter on the pavement.
I went home with scraped, scratched, bleeding knees…
And they spanked me.

Through the tears I saw my father age.
Years of his life poured out of my eyes,
Wetting the knotted rug of their silent bedroom
Where I felt so foreign.

He told me about the life he'd seen…
I wondered how he survives
After so long with a virgin soul.
He's too tired to hear my pains.

If I offer them some,
Will they let me keep it?
The love fell upon me sweetly,
Like the chocolate bar
That melts for years in my mouth…
And I'd give it all to them if they'd take it.

How do they know there's no dope in this candy?
No razor edge in the apple I ate at lunch?
Do they trust me now?
At twenty-three I'm still uncut.
My mouth still has its teeth.
Only my heart is scarred.

But they let me out of sight now.
My skin has grown
Thicker, and nearly opaque.
Bloodless…
Drained into puddles on many floors,
Rugs, stones, sidewalks, and front porches.

I'll sweep up when I'm done.
No trace will remain,
Unless…
Would you like to,,,
Could you….
Share my candy bar?

# Kol Nidrei

*This poem was written while walking home in the dark at the conclusion of the evening service on the "Day of Atonement" my freshman year in college. I had been staring at a burning candle in front of the choir. My emotions combined a sense of being "grown up" yet not quite ready for it (my first holidays away from home). The middle line of the poem is from the prayer book.*

I remember Kol Nidrei
Images of dancing lights and shining stars
Burning in my heart and mind.
Pillars of silvered song, wax tapers,
Pointed outcries --

*With fear and trepidation, yet joy and gladness ringing*

The hand of God
Shapes plastic images
In ways we cannot comprehend.
We never see
Falling like white blankets
Onto golden beds
In winter,
Peaceful sleep.

# A Stone in the Stream

*This poem came to me during a hike in Alaska. Lynda had gone on a more athletic trek across a glacier, leaving me with my camera, my thoughts, and the margins of our tour schedule.*

A stone in the stream
Low-grade copper ore escaped from Kennecott.
You rode the glacier down from the mountains
To pose here, fiercely proud, against the riverbank.
White foam curls in the upstream rapids
Yielding to gray-green silt along the mud flats.
A moment frozen in Nature's time.


A piece of lumber at the water's edge
Ragged one-by-six with nail holes through
Were you once in a cabin roof? A floor?
A crate, long-discarded, miles from here?
Men cut you from the growing tree,
Your tree removed from your native forest.
A moment lost in human time.

# The *Layer-Cake* Country

*This is another poem (see "Zichronot") inspired during a tour of Israel in 2000. I tried to capture the whirlwind of images and emotions I felt during our week in this ancient yet modern land.*

Israel, the layer-cake country…
Civilizations piled one upon the other
Side by side, yet remain distinct
The oil lamp and the cartridge shell,
The pottery shard and the tank grenade,
The bone of a goat and the grave of a child.

Israel, the *melting-pot* country…
A thousand generations of a hundred nations
Within tens of miles…
The longings echo throughout our history
From Babylon to Babi Yar,
Ethiopia to the ghettos of Warsaw.

Israel, the ancient yet modern country…
Older than the Bible stories
And young as the evening CNN report
Where tour buses travel along caravan routes,
Shopping malls share space with native markets,
Archaeologists' sites, and a military museum.

Israel, the long-memoried country…
A history of dates and wars and pain
Assyria, Rome, Greece, Germany
Sharing thoughts with Syria and Lebanon
The graves of Hasmoneans beside those of tank crews,
Seventy BC, and the Yom Kippur war.

Israel, the layer-cake country…
Religions and peoples held together
By a love of the land, history, tradition.
Arab and Christian, Jew and tourist
Meet at the Temple Mount – the "Wall".
Milk and honey – and peace

# Old Blue Jeans

*In chapter 15 in the Book of Numbers, the Hebrews are instructed to "put fringes on the hem of their garments and to put a blue thread on each corner". The fringes are to be visible reminders to obey all the other commandments in the Bible. Commentators have remarked that "to see is to recall, and to recall is to do".*

I ripped the knee of these old blue jeans sliding into home
While scoring the winning run
At the high school softball game
So many years ago.
I've never run so fast in my life.
I'll never forget that feeling.

This splash of white paint came
When re-doing the trim on the second floor
From an old, rickety ladder
That I hadn't braced enough.
I won't make that mistake again.

The front pocket's been replaced three times already
Where my ring of keys wears it through.
The penknife is bulky and it snags the lining
But I never lose it.

The hem on both legs is worn and frayed.
With loose threads that catch on things

When I walk through brushy ground.
I don't do that very much anymore,
But I remember long pleasant walks
In the bright sunshine.

The back pocket has a hole worn through
From years of carrying too large a wallet.
Cards, ID's, and stuff collected along the way
Through a life of joys and some regrets.
These faded jeans hold a lot of memories.

# The Trouble with Corners

*This poem was inspired in 2005. I was reading the line "I will return my people from the four corners of the Earth" in the prayer book.*

There are problems at the corners.
You can't make progress from a corner.
Creativity stops
Lest you step off into the abyss.

There's no room for others at a corner.
A corner's precarious and sharp
Never comfortable
Points leave no margin for safety.

You can't see the world from a corner.
Unless turning back the way you came
And stepping away from the extreme edge
To face towards those standing further in.

Corners are nice as boundaries
Places to think about and look out towards.
So long as we learn to live in the center
Drawing others inward,
And pushing no one out to the fringes.

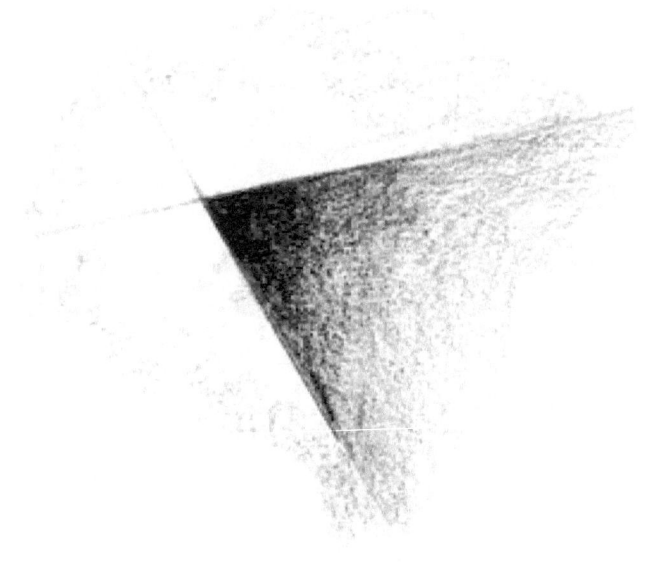

# A Modern "U'va Shofar Godol"

> *This poem is a "modern-day" setting of an ancient prayer from the Hebrew "Day of Atonement" (Yom Kippur) liturgy. (The poem uses a number of "September 11" images.) The prayer takes the form of a communal recognition that the world in which we live is not yet complete, and that we must take our part in the continuing work of creation. The translation begins: "The Great Horn sounds, and a soft voice is heard. Even the angels are afraid, for they, too, fear Divine judgment. We stand like sheep before the Lord, who decides our fate..."*

Sirens of emergency vehicles pierce the sleepy afternoon.
A young child cries outside the ruined restaurant.
The bomb squad is nervous.
"There may still be another one!"
"Somebody saw an old man behind the wall!"
"Don't touch that backpack! It hasn't been checked yet!"
The police stare at each other -- hands clutching their weapons,
While a team of firemen re-coil their hoses.

We form a line outside the checkpoint.
Like sheep, we pass one-by-one through the metal detectors.
The officer in charge carefully eyes each one of us -- we meet his gaze.
Three are taken aside for further questioning.
"Do we dare take the bus back home?"
"Is it safe to attend the outdoor concert tonight?"

*On the "Birthday of the World" humanity was created.*
*And on the "Day of Atonement" our epitaphs are recorded.*

Who by Katyusha rocket, and who by machine-gun bullet.
Who by a suicide bomber, and who by a stray mortar shell.
Who in the collapse of a skyscraper, and who in a plane crash.
Who on a military patrol, and who in a disco.
Who shall have a state funeral, and who shall never be found.
Who in a blinding flash, and who with time to leave a message.
Who for a cause, and who for no discernable reason.

A soft rain falls from leaden skies.
Blood stains wash from the shattered bricks.
The bodies are removed -- the camera crews are gone.
Today's news fades into an old story.

Water and tears feed the parched earth.
The moon and stars look down on all the graves.
Yet, in the morning, the sun rises on a new day,
With another chance at redemption.

# Bible Study

*This poem was written in the aftermath of Hurricane Katrina and the devastating Asian tsunami. The words of eternal hope from the book of Genesis are balanced against the images of destruction and rebirth seen on television around the world.*

*The earth was void and without form…*
*And the voice of the Lord was upon the waters…*

> In the roll of a tsunami wave across the Pacific
> Born of a collapsing mountain deep in the sea
> And in the tidal surge bearing down on Mobile
> Miles ahead of an approaching storm.

*You sweep away people as if they were but a dream.*
*In the morning they are like the new grass.*

> It was no dream to those aboard an oil platform in the Gulf
> Torn from its moorings by a raging sea.
> It was no dream to a family huddled in their attic
> Watching the floodwaters rise.

*But the voice of the Lord was not in the whirlwind.*

> It was not in the flood waters from Lake Pontchartrain.
> It was not in the crashing tidal waves or the leaking levees.

It was not in the spinning devastation of the hurricanes.
Or the incessant pounding of torrential rains.

*God gave Noah the "rainbow sign".*
*Never again will I destroy the world.*

Already life returns, bit by bit, to New Orleans.
Trash-filled streets are cleared, tattered storefronts mended.
Flooded homes pumped clear and families reunited.
Alligators return to their normal homes
While the people rebuild theirs along the waterfront.

*I will gather the exiles from the four corners of the Earth.*

From the Astrodome and Air Force bases,
From Red Cross shelters and tent cities,
And from the homes of strangers.

*And they shall rebuild the waste cities and inhabit them.*
*They shall plant vineyards and drink of their wine.*

The tourist hotels on the beaches of Phuket,
Fishing villages on the shores of Indonesia,
And the bars on Bourbon Street.

*The sound of music and rejoicing shall be heard once more in the land.*

They will celebrate Mardi Gras again on the streets of New Orleans
With the sounds of sweet jazz drifting from the "French Quarter".
Boats shall sail once more from the port of Jakarta
And sailors will look out upon a tranquil sea.

# Conception

*This is an early poem I wrote while watching a snowstorm. I probably should have been doing my homework instead!*

Dark woods
Sulk in moonlight
While white diamonds in the wind
Exhibit their facets to the stars.

Mounded snowdrifts
Roll in from forested land
To bury us in whiteness.

The moon is gone.
Snow has long since melted away.
The trees, having grown to giants,
Now lie sleeping.
Take away your camera!
Consider only the drifting.

# California Sunrise

*This is one of my older poems written during my first trip to California. I was actually in Los Angeles exhibiting software at a computer show, but you never know when the gift of a poem will come. I have noted later that some similar images also appear in another poem "Detroit Metro Fantasy" – also written after an airplane trip.*

The cold dark daylight crouches hunched
On a stool of redwood lumber
While humming soft wind lullabies
Bid sleep a moment longer.
Down behind the mantle shelf
Across the fields of satin floss
Rocky shafts form crimson bars
Against the ever-grays of stars.
In fuzzy, drowsy, morning slumber
The new day dawns,
And rises.

# Sunrise Colors

*This is a more-recent poem (2001) that, like "California Sunrise", was inspired by watching the colors and moods of the dawn – but in a New England winter this time.*

> Gray-green masses of huddled leaves
> Shiver under wet, white blankets.
> Blue ice crystals sparkle a yellow glow
> As sunlight fingers probe and grow.
>
> Glints of rust color paint the tree line.
> Pink blush of morning tints crackling air.
> Orange fire stirs long-slumbering land.
> Which, yawning, rises…
> Day at hand.

# Why I Don't "Get" Jackson Pollock

*This poem came to me during a visit to the Museum of Modern Art in New York City in 2006. While I cite artist Jackson Pollock specifically (there were some seats available in the gallery where his work was exhibited), I really don't understand a lot of the modern "non-representational" art.*

When he starts a new painting,
Canvas stretched taut against the defining frame,
Gesso-coated smooth and even,
Pure and uniform...
How does he begin?

Are his tubes of paint arrayed in careful rows,
Summer colors first – winter colors last?
Is the final result already in his mind,
Or, does it grow organically,
Layer upon layer?

Does he paint all the reds at once,
The blooming roses and spurting blood?
Are the blacks a backdrop for stars
Or a prayer against the coming night?
Is the smear of green a leafy tree?

The blue streaks a sky?
How can he tell?

And, after all the colors are piled up,
And the canvas is awash in paint,
Leaping from the edges of the frame
Ready to crawl across the wall…
All this I can understand in my engineer's heart
But… how does he know when it's done?

This is why I prefer nature to modern art.
God knows we're not finished yet!

# The Evolution of Fear

*This poem was written during a recent cruise vacation in the Galapagos Islands. The teeming abundance of life on these remote islands is remarkable enough, but the total lack of fear exhibited by the animals here was truly amazing. It's easy to see how Charles Darwin might have felt when he visited here and the "theory of evolution" was inspired.*

A remnant of Eden yet remains
Not where you'd expect to find it.
Born from volcanic fire and ocean steam
Six hundred miles west from Ecuador
It's called "Galapagos".

No large predator has evolved on these islands.
No need to run and hide, no need for constant vigilance.
Time for the curiosity of a newborn seal seeing his first tourist.
A boobie chick peeks out of its egg to greet the world.
Iguanas seek sunny spots on the lava rocks
As an albatross takes graceful wing out over the sea
And a pelican dives into crystal water.

They called you "boobie" and "dodo",
Too stupid to flee when man arrived.
You gave yourself freely to the whaler and the pirate
As sustenance for voyages beyond the horizon.

Fresh water to drink, a place to rest,
And you were alone again.

The sea lion swims here with the white-tipped shark.
The penguin fishes side-by-side with the cormorant and the hawk.
Boobies still nest on beaches where lava lizards bask.
Green sea turtles share the seas with rays and frigate birds
And no one makes them afraid.

# Is The Jar Full Yet?

*This poem was inspired by the memory of some first-year physics experiments I used to give my students. Did you ever wonder why the Brazil nuts are usually near the top of the can of mixed nuts and the peanuts are usually near the bottom?*

Take an empty two-quart canning jar
Filled to the brim with your favorite marbles,
"Puries", "steelies", and "cats-eyes"
The precious moments of your life
The victories -- the quiet joys,
The memories that you'll always treasure.
Is the jar full yet?

Take a pail of fine sand from a sea-swept beach
And pour it into your jar of life.
Shake it well as sand grains find their way
Among the marbles – the grit between the good times,
Life's pains and small frustrations,
The losses and the "might have beens".
Is the jar full yet?

Take two cups of fresh coffee – your favorite kind
And pour them into the marbles and sand.
Watch as the liquid takes its place
In the jar you thought was two-times full.
Filtering between the good times and the bad.
Those wonderful moments shared with a friend.
Now it's full!

# A Stain on Stained Glass

*This is my oldest poem in this collection. I wrote it in high school after seeing pictures of the devastated cities in Europe during WWII. It's still one of my favorites.*

The church lies smoldering
Darkened steeple swinging softly on silver threads
Like the bell
Ringed with clashing dust
Where the bomb fell.
Fragments of candles burn in scorched earth holders
Like stars on Heaven's velvet
Burnt iron on velvet altars
In a glass cathedral.
While rings of glimmering glass wedges
Stilettos, lead handled, cleave flesh
Merge with bullets
Flooded with moonlight singing
The chords of angel choirs float clear
Where soft, soft rain touches lead and steel.

# Certainty

*This is one of the newest poems in this collection. I was wondering how some people can be so sure that their actions are justified, even though they cause hurt to so many others.*

I wish I could be absolutely certain…
To know – without any question or doubt,
That whatever I might do tomorrow,
Whoever I might hurt, or whose goals I might delay,
It will all be right and just
And for the "greater good".

I just can't be that secure.
When I wake up tomorrow
(Will I wake up tomorrow?)
Will there be clouds or sun in my new day?
When I look upon the faces of friends and loved ones
Will I know what hides in their innermost thoughts?
When I'm buffeted by countless emotions and urges
Which of them will make a better world?

Of this, I can be certain.
One God created the world I see.
Each wailing baby and each smiling bride
Awakens to this very same sunrise.
We all act our roles in the great play of life,
But none of us has the script to the "final act".

www.ingramcontent.com/pod-product-compliance
Lightning Source LLC
Chambersburg PA
CBHW020337010526
44119CB00001B/13